FOOTBALL SUPERSTARS

DE BRUYNE

RULES

SIMON MUGFORD   DAN GREEN

CONTENTS

FOOTBALL SUPERSTARS

DE BRUYNE
RULES

Hi, pleased to meet you.

We hope you enjoy our book about Kevin De Bruyne!

I'm **VARbot** with all the facts and stats!

SIMON

VAR

4054154

Published in 2021 by Welbeck Children's Books Limited
part of the Welbeck Publishing Group
Offices in: London – 20 Mortimer Street, London W1T 3JW
& Sydney – Level 17, 207 Kent St, Sydney NSW 2000 Australia
Text © 2021 Simon Mugford
Design & Illustration © 2021 Dan Green
ISBN: 978-1-78312-633-0

Writer: Simon Mugford
Designer and Illustrator: Dan Green
Design Manager: Sam James
Senior Commissioning Editor: Suhel Ahmed
Production: Arlene Alexander

A catalogue record for this book is available from the British Library.

Printed in the UK
10 9 8 7 6 5 4 3

Statistics and records correct as of June 2021

CHAPTER 1

BRILLIANT DE BRUYNE

OHHHH, KEVIN DE BRUYNE!

Kevin De Bruyne is an

AWESOME FOOTBALLER.

He is one of the very best in the world. The **Manchester City** man is a **three-time** Premier League champion and an **ABSOLUTE WONDER** in midfield – few players can control a game better than **KDB**.

THIS BOOK IS ALL ABOUT HIM!

WHAT MAKES DE BRUYNE SO GOOD?

Creativity
Full of brilliant ideas to outsmart his opponents.

Dribbling
Simply awesome at getting past defenders with the ball at his feet.

Passing
Delivers excellent, super-accurate passes to his team-mates.

Shooting
Master of the long-range effort.

GOALS and ASSISTS
Kevin is a free-scoring midfielder and one of the BEST assist-providers in the game.

DE BRUYNE IN NUMBERS

How good is De Bruyne? Let's have a look at his numbers:

3 ... PREMIER LEAGUE wins

1 ... FA CUP win

5 ... LEAGUE CUP wins

2 ... PLAYERS' PLAYER OF THE SEASON AWARDS

262 APPEARANCES

67 GOALS

107 ASSISTS for **Manchester City!**

Estimated **£90 MILLION** transfer value

Over **14 MILLION** followers on Instagram!

DE BRUYNE I.D.

NAME: *Kevin De Bruyne*

NICKNAME: *The Ginger Pelé, KDB*

DATE OF BIRTH: *28 June 1991*

PLACE OF BIRTH: *Drongen, Belgium*

HEIGHT: *1.81 m*

POSITION: *Midfielder*

CLUBS: *Genk, Chelsea, Werder Bremen* (on loan), *Wolfsburg, Manchester City*

NATIONAL TEAM: *Belgium*

LEFT OR RIGHT-FOOTED: *Right*

CHAPTER 2

KEVIN DE BOY

Kevin De Bruyne was born in **1991** in Drongen, a town near the city of Ghent in **Belgium.**

Kevin's mum and dad **LOVED** football!

Anna

MASSIVE Liverpool fan

COME ON YOU REDS!

Herwig

Ex-footballer in the Belgian leagues

Kevin started **kicking a ball** as soon as he could walk. He would play with his mum and dad in the **back garden** of their house in Drongen.

Kevin was a natural! His parents knew that he could be a brilliant player.

When he wasn't **playing** football, young Kevin loved to watch it on the TV.

He would sit, **staring at the screen,** carefully studying the game and the players!

He loved English football.

Match of the Day was his favourite programme!

Kevin was a natural with the ball, but his dad helped him develop some proper skills.

He showed him how to **dribble** . . .

He taught him how to **pass** the ball . . .

BOP!

By the time he was **six,** Kevin took his first step to becoming a footballer when he joined his local youth team, **KVV Drongen.**

He wowed the coaches with his **dribbling, passing** and **shooting!**

WHAT A GREAT PLAYER!

His team-mates thought he was

AWESOME.

Except . . . Kevin had a **terrible temper.**
If he couldn't play football, he would cry
and cry until he was red in the face.

When Kevin and his friends played football in a **neighbour's garden,** they kept damaging the flowers.

The neighbour said they could carry on playing, but only if Kevin used his (weaker) **left foot!**

UH-OH!

Oof!

Kevin is **right-footed**, but his left isn't bad either.

Kevin's mum had lived in **England** and she was a **Liverpool fan.** So, Kevin became a Liverpool fan, too!

His favourite player was the striker

Michael Owen.

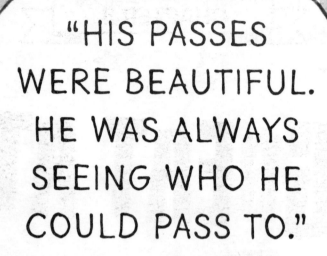

CHAPTER 3

GREAT AT GENT

One **very wet Saturday**, the Drongen pitch was **muddy** and full of puddles, but that didn't bother Kevin!

While the other boys slid around in the mud, Kevin **controlled the game.** He was the **smallest kid** on the pitch - but by far the best.

Jan Van Troos, a scout from the top local side Gent, was amazed!

WE'D LIKE KEVIN TO PLAY FOR **GENT!**

WHOAH!

QUACK!

SPLOTCH!

Kevin trained *part-time* with *Gent,* so that he could still play with his friends in Drongen.

By the time he was 11, Kevin was the **captain** and **star player** of the Gent under-11s.

In **2002,** Gent played Genk in the Belgian **Youth Cup final.** It was a big game at a proper stadium.

The coach knew how to get the best from Kevin, and told him he would **start on the bench.**

GRRR!

Kevin was **furious!**

Then, the coach brought Kevin on after two

minutes . . . and he scored

FOUR goals as

Gent won **6-2**.

BOOM!

At the youth cup final, Kevin proved that he was a **future star** – on and off the pitch.

Like a true pro, he gave **TV interviews** before and after the game.

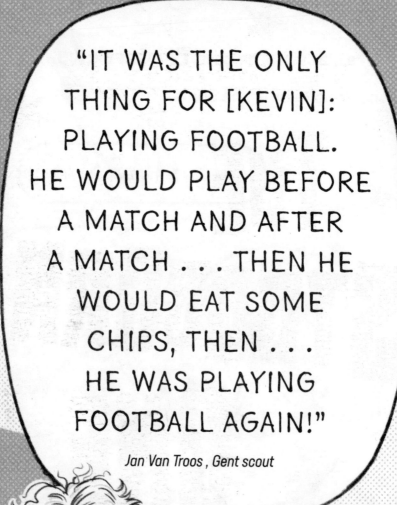

"IT WAS THE ONLY THING FOR [KEVIN]: PLAYING FOOTBALL. HE WOULD PLAY BEFORE A MATCH AND AFTER A MATCH . . . THEN HE WOULD EAT SOME CHIPS, THEN . . . HE WAS PLAYING FOOTBALL AGAIN!"

Jan Van Troos, Gent scout

36

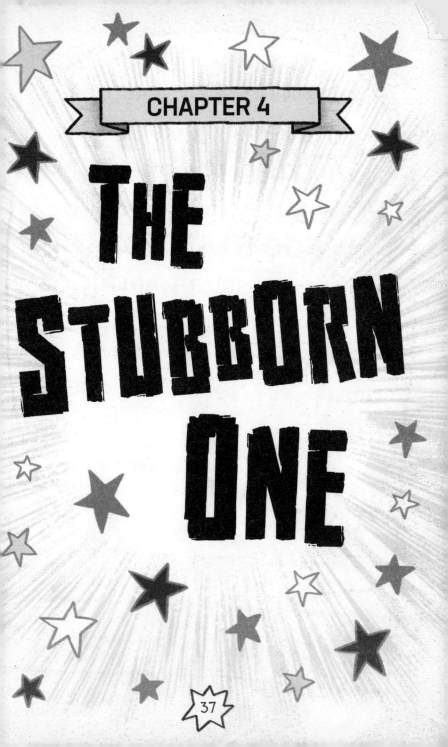

CHAPTER 4

THE STUBBORN ONE

When he was **11,** Kevin had written his own plan for his future.

MY FOOTBALL PLAN
BY KEVIN DE BRUYNE, AGED II

I. Now I will play for Gent and study hard at school (even in my Latin classes).

EGO AMARE EU*

*I love football

2. When I'm 14, I will go to sports school.

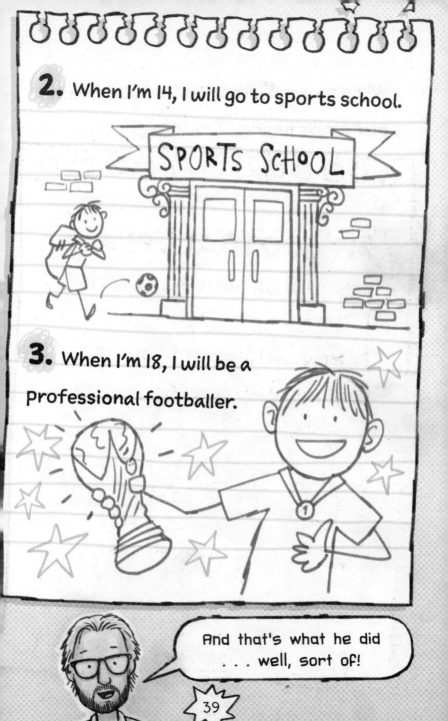

SPORTS SCHOOL

3. When I'm 18, I will be a professional footballer.

And that's what he did . . . well, sort of!

Kevin is a very **chilled-out** and **super-cool** guy. But on the pitch . . . he can be very different.

At a tournament with Gent, Kevin sat down in the **middle of the pitch** when the team lost.

GRRR!

At a training camp, Kevin refused to help clear up, and **held on to the goalpost,** refusing to move!

That stubborn boy grew up to become a determined pro. De Bruyne is **100% focused** on everything he does.

His **decision-making** is unbeatable.

On the pitch, he makes the **best passes . . .**

Scores **important goals** . . .

And is **not afraid** to tell his team-mates

what they need to do!

PUSH FORWARD LADS!

While Kevin was developing as a player at Gent, he discovered a **new footballing idol.**

The French midfielder **Zinedine Zidane** was playing in his prime at **Real Madrid.**

The young Kevin was amazed by **'Zizou'**.

"I WILL BE JUST LIKE ZIDANE"

45

"THERE ARE ALWAYS NEW CHALLENGES IN FOOTBALL. YOU JUST NEED TO ADAPT; OTHERWISE, YOU WON'T FIT IN. AND IF YOU DON'T FIT IN, THEN YOU WILL HAVE TO GO SOMEWHERE ELSE."

Kevin De Bruyne

CHAPTER 5

GOING TO GENK

Kevin was always looking for a **new challenge.**
So, in **2005,** he moved 150 km from home to
join . . . **Genk!**

GENK ARE THE CLUB FOR ME.

48

It was a **big move** for a 14-year-old. But Kevin didn't mind - he was living with his team-mates and having **lots of fun!**

Dan, did you know that Genk are known as *The Smurfs?*

Really?

Kevin was still **NOT** a big fan of training . . .

But he quickly became Genk's **best academy player.** And his team-mates liked him because he created so many **goals** for them!

At 16, De Bruyne was playing in the Genk **under-21s.** He had a great partnership with striker **Christian Benteke** - Kevin set the goals up and Benteke **scored** them!

POW!

At **17,** Kevin started training with the **first team.** The players could not believe it when the **quiet, blond-haired kid** started shouting and telling them what to do!

COME ON LADS!

Kevin made his senior debut at the end of the
2008–09 season against **Charleroi.**

He came on as a sub and only played nine

minutes, but that was enough – he was now

a professional footballer.

GENK GAMES

SOME OF KEVIN'S KEY MATCHES WITH **THE SMURFS**.

7 FEBRUARY 2010

BELGIAN PRO LEAGUE

GENK 1-0 STANDARD LIÈGE

Kevin scored his **first professional goal** in this match as he became a key member of the Genk team.

54

8 AUGUST 2010

BELGIAN PRO LEAGUE

GENT 0-4 GENK

*Kevin **opened the scoring** in this early-season visit to his old club.*

BOOM!

15 AUGUST 2010

BELGIAN PRO LEAGUE

GENK 5-0 CHARLEROI

*Kevin scored **two goals** and assisted another in this big home win.*

CHAMPIONS!

In the **2010–11** season, Kevin's **FIVE** goals and 16 assists in the league helped Genk win the Belgian **championship.**

It was Genk's first league title for **nine years!**

The following season, Kevin scored a hat-trick against Club Brugge. He was the next big thing – **where would he go next?**

DE BRUYNE'S ALL COMPETITIONS GENK RECORD

SEASON	GAMES	GOALS	ASSISTS
2008-09	2	-	-
2009-10	40	3	4
2010-11	35	6	17
2011-12	36	8	15

Cool! Can I take the Smurf costume off now?

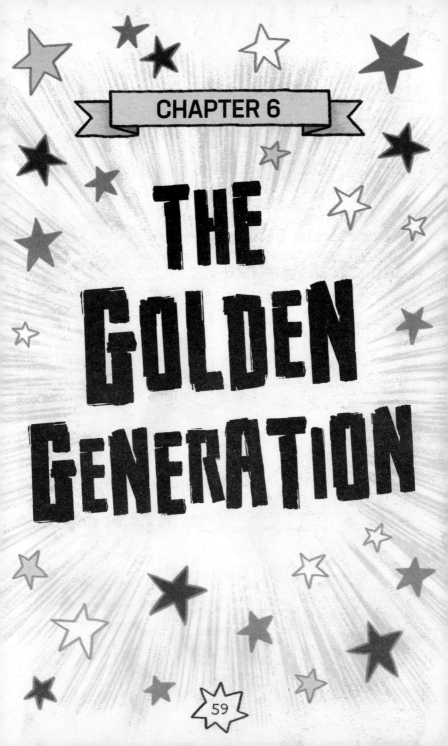

CHAPTER 6

THE GOLDEN GENERATION

De Bruyne made his international debut in **2010.** He joined a **Golden Generation** of brilliant Belgian players including:

Kevin's former Genk team-mate **Christian Benteke** . . .

Manchester City legend **Vincent Kompany** . . .

Wing wizard **Eden Hazard** . . .

OUT NOW!

Sensational striker

Romelu Lukaku.

In **2012,** qualifying began for the **2014 World Cup.** Belgium had not been to a major tournament for **10 years!**

Kevin scored his **first international goal** in a crucial tie against **Serbia.**

He scored **three more times** - and assisted for four - as Belgium easily won the group.

THE BELGIANS WERE GOING TO BRAZIL!

WORLD CUP 2014

At the tournament in **Brazil,** Belgium **topped the group** and faced the **USA** in the **round of 16.**

The match went to extra-time . . . and then ***BOOM*** - Kevin scored his first ever World Cup finals goal!

BOFF!

Then he set one up for Lukaku to secure a place in the **quarter-final** against **Argentina.**

Belgians around the world celebrated their country's best World Cup since *1986!*

But they did lose to Argentina.

EURO 2016

10 OCTOBER 2015

EURO 2016 QUALIFYING GROUP H

ANDORRA 1-4 BELGIUM

Kevin scored one of the four goals in a win that secured qualification for **EURO 2016**. Belgium eventually finished **top of the group.**

De Bruyne and Eden Hazard were Belgium's **joint-top scorers** in qualifying, with **five goals** each.

26 JUNE 2016

EURO 2016 ROUND OF 16

HUNGARY 0-4 BELGIUM

*Belgium dominated this knock-out game, with De Bruyne assisting for **two** of the goals.*

The team unfortunately went out to Wales

in the **quarter-finals.**

67

WORLD CUP WONDER GOAL

6 JULY 2018

WORLD CUP QUARTER-FINAL

BRAZIL 1-2 BELGIUM

A World Cup quarter-final against Brazil? What a **MASSIVE** game! Belgium took the lead through an early own goal, then on the half-hour mark, Lukaku played the ball to Kevin and . . . **POW** – he sent it flying into the goal - **a real netbuster!**

Belgium beat England *twice* at the 2018 World Cup.

68

Kevin's determination to get Belgium to tournaments continued on the way to **EURO 2020.** He scored **FOUR** times and provided **SEVEN** assists during qualification.

CAPS	GOALS	ASSISTS
80	21	38

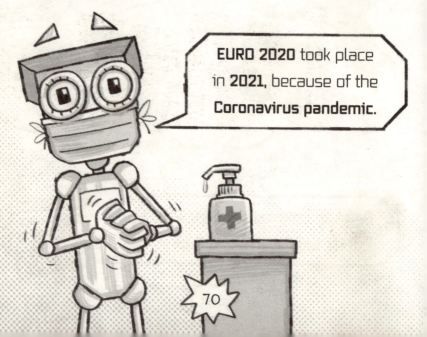

EURO 2020 took place in **2021,** because of the **Coronavirus pandemic.**

CHAPTER 7

LONDON AND LOANS

In early 2012, the BIG boss of **Chelsea, Roman Abramovich** saw a video of Kevin in action and called the club manager.

And with that, for around

£7 MILLION,

Kevin was off to London.

For the **2012–13 season,** Chelsea sent Kevin on loan again. This time, he was going to **Germany** to play for the **Bundesliga** side **Werder Bremen.**

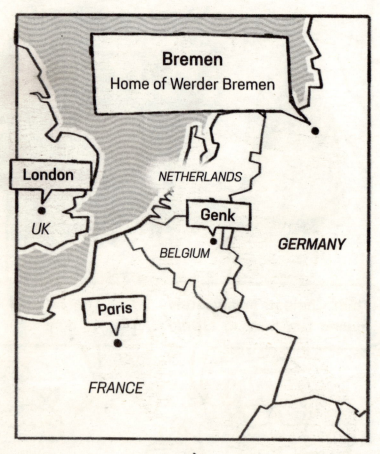

Bremen
Home of Werder Bremen

London
UK

NETHERLANDS

Genk

BELGIUM

GERMANY

Paris

FRANCE

There was **no place** for him at Chelsea, but Kevin would show them what they were missing!

And he did . . .

Werder Bremen were fighting relegation

for most of the season.

But De Bruyne was

AWESOME!

He scored **10 goals**

and provided **NINE**

assists in the

league to help them

avoid the drop.

Jürgen Klopp was the **Borussia Dortmund** manager at the time. He was ready to sign Kevin.

Kevin was named **Young Bundesliga Player of the Year.**

When Kevin finally played for Chelsea, he made his **Premier League debut** against **Hull City.** But then he spent more time on the bench than on the pitch.

Kevin had had enough.

It was time to move on!

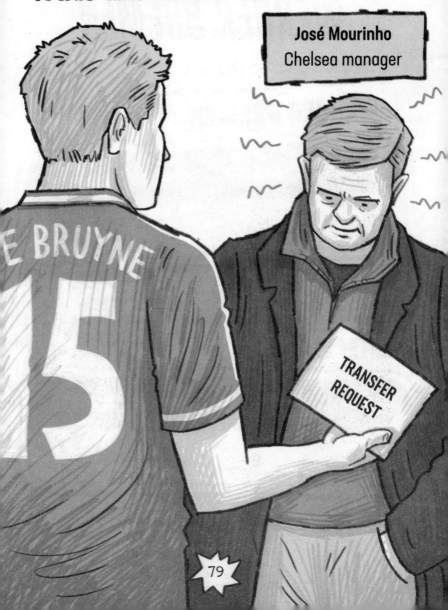

José Mourinho
Chelsea manager

E BRUYNE

15

TRANSFER
REQUEST

KEVIN AT CHELSEA AND WERDER BREMEN

WERDER BREMEN

SEASON	GAMES	GOALS	ASSISTS
2012-13	34	10	10

CHELSEA

SEASON	GAMES	GOALS	ASSISTS
2012-13	9	-	1

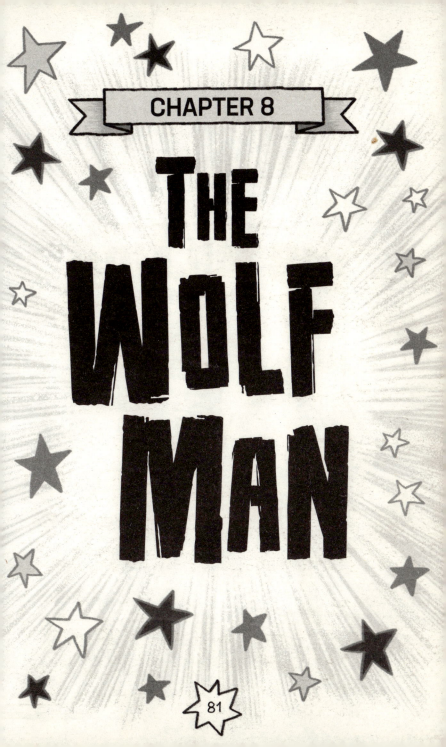

CHAPTER 8

THE WOLF MAN

De Bruyne felt at home in the Bundesliga, so in **January 2014**, he said cheerio to Chelsea and joined **Wolfsburg** for a club record fee of

£18 MILLION.

In the 16 games he played in the **2013–14** season in the **Bundesliga,** Kevin assisted **SIX times** and scored **three goals.**

He was on the up!

Wolfsburg are known as *'The Wolves'*

KING OF THE ASSISTS

SOME HIGHLIGHTS OF KEVIN'S RECORD-BREAKING FIRST FULL SEASON AT WOLFSBURG.

30 JANUARY 2015

WOLFSBURG 4-1 BAYERN MUNICH

At home to a Bayern side managed by **Pep Guardiola,** The Wolves were 1-0 up after just **FOUR minutes** thanks to a De Bruyne pass. He then went on to score **TWICE**. Class!

Later, Pep tried to sign Kevin for Bayern.

1 MARCH 2015

WERDER BREMEN 3-5 WOLFSBURG

*Kevin set up **THREE** of Wolfsburg's **five goals** in this thriller against his old club. **WOW!***

Kevin's **21 league assists** in 2014-15 was a Bundesliga record.

In a brilliant **3–1** win against **Inter Milan** in the **Europa League**, Kevin was involved in all **THREE** goals, scoring two and assisting the other.

KA-POW!

De Bruyne scored the second goal in a 3-1 **German Cup Final** win over Jürgen Klopp's **Borussia Dortmund.** It was the first time Wolfsburg had lifted the trophy in their history.

Wolfsburg finished second in the Bundesliga and qualified for the **Champions League.**

It was Wolfsburg's **most successful** season **EVER** – and Kevin was at the heart of it.

Kevin's success won him the **Bundesliga Footballer of the Year** award in 2015.

DE BRUYNE'S WOLFSBURG RECORD

SEASON	GAMES	GOALS	ASSISTS
2013-14	18	3	7
2014-15	51	16	28
2015-16	4	1	2

CHAPTER 9

PREMIER PLAYMAKER

Kevin left Wolfsburg at the start of the
2015–16 season to head back to England
and the **Premier League.**

This time, he would wear the sky blue shirt of

MANCHESTER CITY.

DE BRUYNE

17

90

And as the club's **record £55 million signing,** he was unlikely to sit on the bench like he did at Chelsea!

Kevin was joining a massively successful

team with brilliant players, such as:

Exciting English winger

Raheem Sterling

Another new signing

Super Argentine striker

Sergio Agüero

Awesome Spanish midfielder **David Silva**

City's Belgian captain **Vincent Kompany**

A familiar face!

2015-16 HIGHLIGHTS

THE BEST BITS OF DE BRUYNE'S DEBUT SEASON AT MAN CITY.

3 OCTOBER 2015

PREMIER LEAGUE

**MANCHESTER CITY 6
NEWCASTLE UNITED 1**

Kevin's goal was his **THIRD** *in* **THREE** *games and the Assist King also set up two of Agüero's* **FIVE** *goals.* **BOOM!**

BLAM!

27 JANUARY 2016

EFL CUP SEMI-FINAL, 2ND LEG

MANCHESTER CITY 3-1 EVERTON

*It was 1-1 when Kevin came on as sub in the 70th minute. A **goal** and an **assist** from him sent City to the final!*

12 APRIL 2016

CHAMPIONS LEAGUE QUARTER-FINAL 2ND LEG

MANCHESTER CITY 1
PARIS SAINT-GERMAIN 0

*Kevin scored the **only goal** to send City to their first ever **Champions League semi-final**.*

DE BRUYNE'S DEBUT SEASON RECORD

GAMES	GOALS	ASSISTS
41	16	13

"SOMETIMES ONE PLAYER CAN CHANGE A TEAM."

Ex-Man City manager Manuel Pellegrini on De Bruyne

CHAPTER 10

THE PEP EFFECT

City's new manager for the **2016–17** season was **Pep Guardiola.** Pep had won **La Liga** and the **Champions League** with **Barcelona** and three Bundesliga titles at **Bayern Munich.**

BREAKING NEWS! Pep Guardiola is the new Manager at Man City.

DERBY DELIGHT

10 SEPTEMBER 2016

PREMIER LEAGUE

MANCHESTER UNITED 1
MANCHESTER CITY 2

The fourth league game of the season was a
BIG ONE - away to big rivals Man United
and their new manager, Kevin's old boss,
José Mourinho. Kevin opened the scoring
after **15 minutes** and City won 2-1!

JOSÉ

PEP

VS

José was not happy!

Pep and **José** had been *big rivals* in Spain when Mourinho was the manager of **Real Madrid.**

De Bruyne went on to notch up **seven goals** and a fantastic **21 assists** in all competitions that season.

Things just got **better and better** for

Kevin in **2017–18** when he

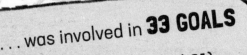

. . . was involved in **33 GOALS**

(scored 12, assisted 21)

. . . scored against **Chelsea, Arsenal** and **Tottenham**

. . . won the **League Cup final** against **Arsenal**

. . . was named **Premier League Playmaker of the Year,** for the most assists

. . . and was voted **Manchester City's Player of the Season.**

103

RECORD CHAMPIONS

13 MAY 2018

PREMIER LEAGUE

SOUTHAMPTON 0

MANCHESTER CITY 1

It was the last day of the season and City had already **won the league.** Deep into injury time, Kevin passed to Gabriel Jesus – who scored!

BOFF!

The win meant City had

100 POINTS

- the most ever in the English top flight!

DE BRUYNE AND MAN CITY WERE FLYING HIGH!

DE BRUYNE'S 2017-18 RECORD

GAMES	GOALS	ASSISTS
52	12	21

"I'M A CREATOR AND I TRY TO CREATE CHANCES FOR MY TEAM-MATES. IF THEY SCORE, I GET THE ASSIST AND I LOOK GOOD!"

Kevin De Bruyne

CHAPTER 11

MAN CITY MAN

2018-19 started out badly for Kevin. He injured his **right knee** in training and missed the first **THREE MONTHS** of the season.

Soon after he came back, he injured his **left knee!**

But he scored on the way to City's **League Cup win** and provided **THREE assists** in a 4-3 Champions League quarter-final win against Spurs.

CRACK!

Spurs actually won this on away goals.

Meanwhile, City won their **second Premier League title** under Pep Guardiola.

TREBLE TRIUMPH

18 MAY 2019

FA CUP FINAL

MANCHESTER CITY 6-0 WATFORD

De Bruyne was a second-half substitute.

Just **six minutes** after coming on, he had scored City's **third goal.**

Seven minutes later he set **Gabriel Jesus** up for the fourth.

BOOM!

Watford were finished, leaving City with a historic **TREBLE win.**

IT WAS A *FANTASTIC* END TO A DIFFICULT SEASON FOR KEVIN.

It was the **first** domestic **treble** in English football.

The following season, Kevin assisted **EIGHT** times in the first **SEVEN** league games . . .

. . . and scored **13 PREMIER LEAGUE** goals, including strikes against **Chelsea, Arsenal** and eventual title winners **Liverpool.**

Kevin's form continued despite the *season break* for the *Coronavirus pandemic.*

His **20 Premier League assists** won him the **Playmaker of the Season Award.**

He was named Premier League Player of the Season **AND** the PFA Player of the Year.

PREMIER PROVIDERS

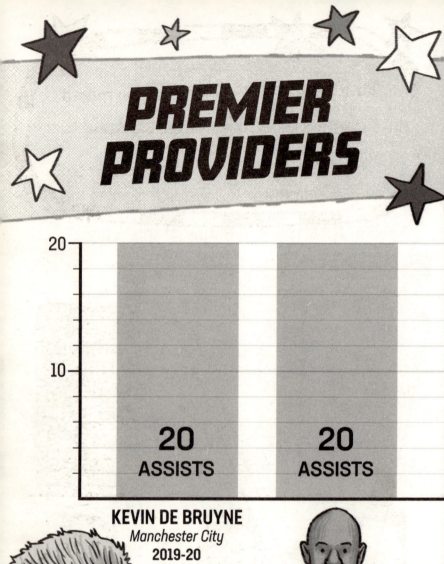

20 ASSISTS

20 ASSISTS

KEVIN DE BRUYNE
Manchester City
2019-20

THIERRY HENRY
Arsenal
2002-03

114

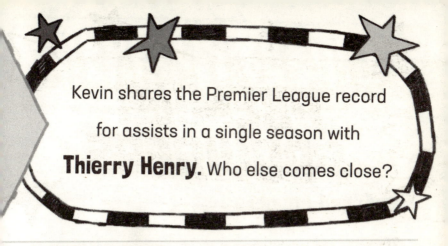

Kevin shares the Premier League record for assists in a single season with **Thierry Henry.** Who else comes close?

19 ASSISTS	**18** ASSISTS	**15** ASSISTS

MESUT ÖZIL
Arsenal
2015-16

FRANK LAMPARD
Chelsea
2005-06

DAVID BECKHAM
Manchester United
1999-00

KING PLAYMAKERS

Kevin is up there with some of the world's greatest playmakers for all-time assists for **club and country:**

KEVIN DE BRUYNE
MANCHESTER CITY / BELGIUM

566 GAMES

227 ASSISTS

ASSISTS PER GAME **0.40**

LIONEL MESSI
BARCELONA / ARGENTINA

913 GAMES

342 ASSISTS

ASSISTS PER GAME **0.37**

THOMAS MÜLLER
BAYERN MUNICH / GERMANY

677
GAMES

251
ASSISTS

ASSISTS PER GAME **0.37**

CRISTIANO RONALDO
JUVENTUS / PORTUGAL

1016
GAMES

268
ASSISTS

ASSISTS PER GAME **0.25**

Kevin continued to be **AWESOME** in **2020–21.** Wearing the captain's armband, he led City all the way to their first **Champions League final.**

Unfortunately, City lost to **Chelsea** - and De Bruyne was injured.

But he did win his *THIRD* Premier League title as City were crowned champions again!

DE BRUYNE'S MAN CITY RECORD

SEASON	GAMES	GOALS	ASSISTS
2015-16	41	16	13
2016-17	49	7	21
2017-18	52	12	21
2018-19	32	6	11
2019-20	48	16	23
2020-21	40	10	18

De Bruyne signed a new **four-year contract** with City in 2021.

He negotiated the contract himself (with his lawyers)!

The brilliant Belgian will continue to thrill

City fans and light up the Premier League -

DE BRUYNE RULES!

KEVIN'S HONOURS AND AWARDS

DE BRUYNE'S MAJOR ACHIEVEMENTS (SO FAR)

PREMIER LEAGUE
2017-18
2018-19
2020-21

FA CUP
2018-19

EFL CUP
2015-16
2017-18
2018-19
2019-20
2020-21

BELGIAN PRO LEAGUE
2010-11

GERMAN CUP
2014-15

BUNDESLIGA
YOUNG PLAYER OF
THE YEAR
2012-13

BUNDESLIGA
PLAYER OF THE
YEAR
2014-15

MAN CITY PLAYER
OF THE SEASON
2015-16
2017-18
2019-20

PREMIER LEAGUE
PLAYER OF THE
SEASON
2019-20

PFA PLAYER OF
THE YEAR
2019-20
2020-21

123

QUIZ TIME!

How much do you know about **KEVIN DE BRUYNE?** Try this quiz to find out, then test your friends!

1. Which team does Kevin's mum support?

----

2. What was Kevin's favourite TV programme as boy?

----

3. Which team did Kevin win the Belgian Youth Cup Final with?

----

4. What is Genk's nickname?

----

5. Which team did Belgium beat in the 2018 World Cup quarter-final?

----

6. How much did Chelsea pay for De Bruyne in 2012?

----

7. How many assists did De Bruyne make in the Bundesliga in 2014-15?

----

8. How many goals did De Bruyne score for Man City in his debut season?

----

9. How many points did Man City finish on in 2017-18?

----

10. How many times has Kevin won the Premier League with City?

The answers are on the next page *but no peeking!*

ANSWERS

1. Liverpool

2. Match of the Day

3. Gent

4. The Smurfs

5. Brazil

6. £7 Million

7. 21

8. 16

9. 100

10. Three

KEVIN DE BRUYNE:
WORDS YOU NEED TO KNOW

Belgian Pro League
The top football league in Belgium.

Bundesliga
The top football league in Germany.

Champions League
European club competition. The winner is the best team in Europe.

EFL Cup
The second English knockout cup competition.

FA Cup
The top English knockout cup competition.

Premier League
The top football league in England.

ABOUT THE AUTHORS

Simon's first job was at the Science Museum, making paper aeroplanes and blowing bubbles big enough for your dad to stand in. Since then he's written all sorts of books about the stuff he likes, from dinosaurs and rockets, to llamas, loud music and of course, football. Simon has supported Ipswich Town since they won the FA Cup in 1978 (it's true - look it up) and once sat next to Rio Ferdinand on a train. He lives in Kent with his wife and daughter, a dog, cat and two tortoises.

Dan has drawn silly pictures since he could hold a crayon. Then he grew up and started making books about stuff like trucks, space, people's jobs, *Doctor Who* and *Star Wars*. Dan remembers Ipswich Town winning the FA Cup but he didn't watch it because he was too busy making a Viking ship out of brown paper. As a result, he knows more about Vikings than football. Dan lives in Suffolk with his wife, son, daughter and a dog that takes him for very long walks.